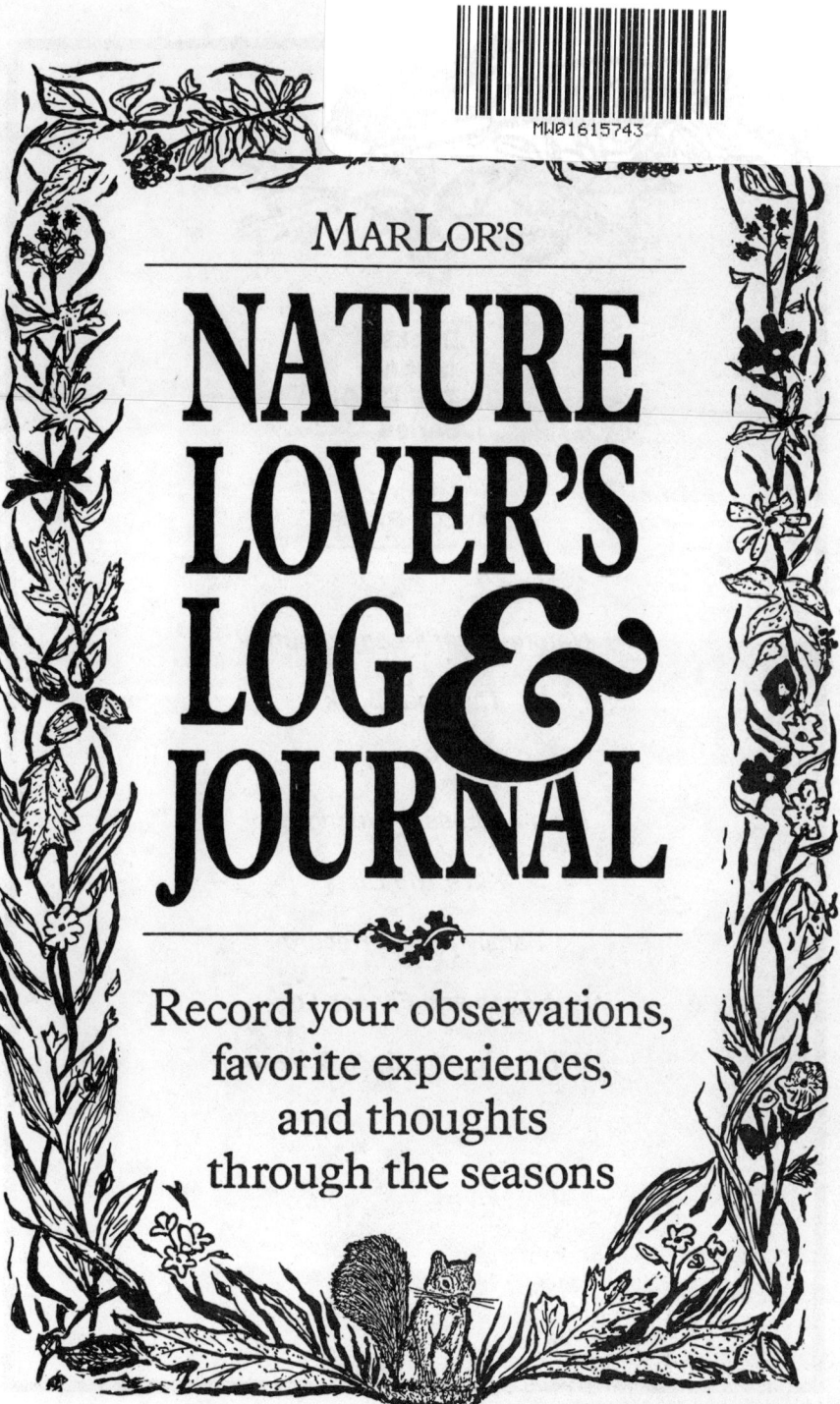

MARLOR'S

NATURE LOVER'S LOG & JOURNAL

Record your observations,
favorite experiences,
and thoughts
through the seasons

**Books
in the
GIFTEE BOOK** tm
Series

from
MARLOR PRESS:

Nature Lover's Log & Journal

The Boat Book

Complete Trip Diary

Kid's Address & Writing Book

Kid's Trip Diary

Family Health Record

Health and Fitness Log

Holiday Memory Book & Record

MARLOR'S

NATURE LOVER'S LOG & JOURNAL

ML

MARLOR PRESS

Nature Lover's Log & Journal. Published by MarLor
Press. All rights reserved, including the right of
reproduction in whole or in any part in any form.

A MarLor Press **Giftee Book**

Illustrations by Marlin Bree

Distributed to the book trade by:
Contemporary Books / 180 North Michigan Avenue/
Chicago, Illinois   60601 / Telephone (312) 782-9181

First Printing: August, 1990

Printed in the United States of America

ISBN 0-943400-50-3

ML

MARLOR PRESS

4304 Brigadoon Dr ./ St. Paul, MN   55126 / (612) 484-4600

CONTENTS

CONTENTS

HOW TO ENJOY
THIS BOOK

Welcome to the wonderful world of nature.

This book can help you get **more enjoyment** out of your time out in our natural world, whether you are a casual observer and occasional field explorer—or a dedicated bird watcher.

It can help you learn more about your observations by letting you systematically **record** what you see. This is significant because an important process takes place: you begin to **think about** and **sort through** the sometimes bewildering, if fascinating, spectrum of natural events.

Soon, **patterns** will form and **connections** will fit together like pieces in a picture puzzle. Your understanding and knowledge will grow—as will your *appreciation* and *love*.

A PERSPECTIVE

With this book, you join the ranks of many **others** who have kept a nature log or journal. These range from famous naturalists, such as **Charles Darwin**, who set his observations down with great care, to people who just have had an interest in their own backyard and keep a log for their own personal satisfaction. Your observations may not shake the natural world, but you can have a **lot of fun** keeping your own records.

Enjoyment is a process that can extend to *others*. For a family, keeping a log can lead to many conversations and family projects, such as further observations or extended field expeditions as family vacations. You may even want to start your own backyard wildlife project.

But above all, a log is personally **satisfying**. A famous novelist once observed that writing lets us "taste life *twice*---first in the *living* of it, then in the *telling*."

We can live again in the pages we have kept, recalling many fine **memories**. And for that matter, by writing things down, we keep a record for others who may follow us, such as our younger generations.

By keeping a log, we enter a process which lets us **focus** in on our lives with more *clarity and detail*. We see not only the world around us emerging, but through the patterns we see **ourselves**, and parts of our lives.

A journal is in part **discovery**—of the world about us, and of *ourselves*.

HOW THIS BOOK
IS ORGANIZED

This book is divided into four sections:

1/ How to use this book
2/ Your log and journal
3/ Summary details
4/ Additional notes

The **first section** tells you some of the things you can do
with your log and journal. Here you can learn specifically
what your log can contain as well as some of the things you

can begin to **look for**. With this help, you can find a place and a way to begin your log, whether you are a beginner or an expert.

The **second section** contains your **log and journal**, enough for **many observations** and happy hours of recording. Here is space for the essentials of your observation, including the subject, date, location, and the specific information of your observation. You can make each as short or as lengthy as you wish.

Summary Details gives you a chance to **organize** categories you are interested in, such as bird sightings. Here you can write down details of the birds you have seen, when you have seen them, at what location, their coloration, unusual markings, or any other details you may wish.

Finally, a **Notes section** lets you jot down your own questions or special observations, including research details you might like to look up at a later date.

All in all, you can build up a **wealth of detail** in this journal as well as a fine storehouse of memories. Remember, too, that in keeping your journal, you are not writing to have a finished piece of literature. Just jot down what **you see** and **feel,** and your writings can be as short or as long as you feel like.

The important things is **to begin**---and **keep it up.** And *enjoy!*

SECTION 1

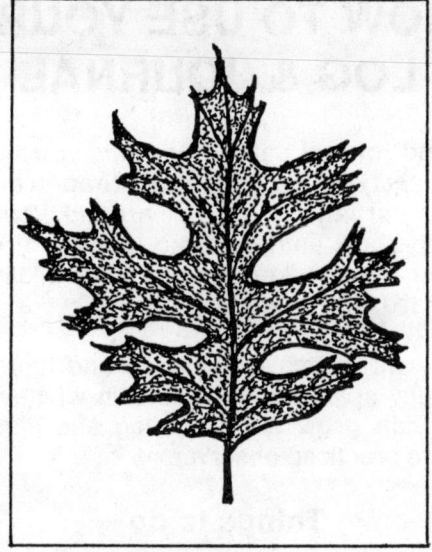

**How to use your
Log & Journal**

What to look for

Log entries

HOW TO USE YOUR
LOG & JOURNAL

Your **log and journal** can be *anything* **you** *want it* to be. That's the *beauty* of it. You can keep track of your day-to-day observations in and around your backyard birdfeeder with **short** entries, make **longer** entries during a nature hike, or even make a **pages-long** wildlife notebook after an extended stay or encampment.

Anyway you want to use it, your log and journal lets you record the many splendors of nature in whatever way you want to. You can **grow** with your log and journal as you become a more practiced observer.

Things to do

The **next chapter** gives you some insights into what to look for. You can: *Keep a daily list and later a lifelist of all the birds you sight *Watch for backyard squirrel or other wildlife antics *Observe the cycle of life around you *Visit a lake, pond or water hole and have an adventure recording all that you see *Take a nature hike, row around a lake, or an extended vacation *Just plain have a good time looking, sharpening your instincts---and learning

What to write:

In your **Log & Journal,** you will see two columns: A **short** one on the **left** and a **longer** one on the **right**

The **left hand column** is for your **subject heading** and date. Make these **short,** so that they become easy-to-identify for you. For example:

SUBJECT & DATE   NOTES

Be sure to add a **date.**

Cardinal _____
7 – 16 _____

On the **right hand side**, you will see a long series of lines. Use as many of these, or as few, as you need to make your log or journal entry. Use pages, if you like.

Cardinal   At feeder 7:30a.m.
7-16   Got a seed + flew off
Large male bird.

And when you're ready to start **another entry**, just leave a **space**, and begin all over again with the subject and date on the short, left hand column, and your observation in the right hand column. Like this:

Woods   Took a walk in the north woods.
4/12   Everything is green. Found small
white trillium with narrow
leaves. It was a Snow trillium

Storm   It stormed last night. Only the
4/14   willow lost branches. Everything
was very quiet when I got up, but
within an hour the birds were back
at the feeder. Two rabbits were
playing in the back yard.

Easy, isn't it? Now you can have **as much space** to write in as you need—or, for that matter, you can make your observations as compact as you want.

In **Section 2**, you can develop an **index** to your notes and a **list** of all of the different and interesting items you have recorded. For example, you may wish to list the first time you see a new bird or each time you see something new.

WHAT TO LOOK FOR

Weather:

Descriptions:

sunny
cloudy

**Temperature
comparisons:**

cooler, warmer
statistics- degrees
freezing,
hot, cold, cool, warm
fog
snow
rain: amount, hard,
gentle etc.
sleet
hail

humidity:

high
low
percent

thunder / lightning:

thunderstorms / high winds
branches broken
lightning strikes

Other storms:

hurricanes
tornados

pressure

high/low

rising/falling
tides

How weather affects nature:

blows down trees
grass turns brown / green
wildlife appears,
disappears etc.

Sky:

Clouds
clear
color
halo around sun/moon
full moon, quarter moon
stars
aurora borealis
meteor showers

Birds:

where sighted
specific type of habitat :
   (grassland, coniferous or deciduous forest, desert, swamp etc.)
time of year
type of weather
in group or alone
migrating or permanent
resident
if this is an *unusual sighting* , is it possible to get a photo

color

note wings, tail, back,
breast, crown, head, throat, bill
is it striped, plain
differences in color
wing bars -- how many
any contrasting colors?

shape

fat or thin
neck, legs, tail -- long or short
shape of tail
shape of head, does it have crest?
how do the wings appear when in flight?

overall appearance

size *(compare to another more familiar bird like a robin or a sparrow)*
bill *(short or chunky, rounded or pointed, color, straight or curved)*

voice

note calls or songs heard

Flowers, plants

Plants:

where does it grow

Characteristics:

stem:
does it branch

where does it branch --
top or bottom
  height
  where are leaves and
flowers attached *(all at one
place or at several sites)*

leaves:

  compound (divided)
like a palm or like a
feather
  simple (not divided)
  shape
  edges
plain, toothed or lobed
  placement on the stem
    (two opposite each other
    more than two at a point
    only one at a point)
  smooth, prickly, fuzzy etc.

Flowers:

color:

  specific colors
  pale or dark

petals:
  how many
  separate or joined
  shape *(funnel, bowl,
saucer, etc.)*

ovary *(the part that
produces the fruit):*

  position
  in the center or at the
bottom
  where attached

stamens:

  appearance

sepals:

  appearance

shape:

  number of parts
  symmetry

Animals

Size
Shape
Color of fur
Pawprints--size, number
of toe or claws, direction of
movement
  Calls or sounds
  Head shape & color
  Ears
  Tail
  Motion, posture or action
  Reactions to environment
or stimulus
  Male or female
  Attitude or body language

General

These are **some** of the
ways you can observe and
record the **natural world**
about you. As you become
more skilled, you can
develop additional infor-
mation. You also can add to
your knowledge through
books on nature or wildlife
watching.

Log & Journal
ENTRIES

Subjects

Dates

Notes

OBSERVATIONS
NOTES

SUBJECT & DATE

4/1/94	On our way to the WA. coast with Jim, Rob & Jesse, left Lynden 4:45 arrived at
grayland WA	grayland at 9:00PM. Trip felt like it went really fast. Watched 3 Stooges from 10:30 - 11:30. Nice one bedroom cabin, sparsely furnished.
4/2/94	All up by 6:30AM On beach by 7:45 AM! 8:15 Jim & I back in cabin, left boys on beach to play. low tide today at 11:30AM. Cloudy Day - about 45-50°
Sandpipers	Saw Sandpipers running fast on beach & inserting their bills into the sand, then running again to next spot - about 50 of them on the beach. A flock of about 100 ducks flew overhead. There are 2 ponds between cabins and the sand dunes - full of mosquitos, frogs (croaks in unison - greeted us last night

SUBJECT & DATE	NOTES
	on our arrival) Jesse said he saw a red wing blackbird. There's a pair of dock like birds on the lake - not sure what type.
4·3·94	Went South six miles to a long beach - Jesse and Jim did some surf fishing. The wind was blowing strong out of the NW - I'd say about 35 mph. Then it rained hard for about 15 minutes. Rob jumped waves - I walked between them all, and chatted breifly. We were gone about 2 hours - Cold and wet, we came home. (We had a picnic lunch on the beach). Made tortellini for dinner w/ salad, peaches, bread & butter. Rob and Jesse did the dishes, wiped the table and made their bed. Lights out at 11:30.
4.4.94	We got up between 9 & 10 AM - a nice calm, relaxing A.M., each person eating and getting dressed at their leisure.

OBSERVATIONS

SUBJECT & DATE

NOTES

4.4.94 Today was far less stormy than yesterday, so we decided to go whale watching from 2-4:30, we were out! Took the BOAT - DELUXE - an 80 ft. motor boat, $19.50 for adults, $11.50 for kids - about $67.00 for all of us! We saw several whales - California Whales, I in the area between jetty's and several about 2 miles off shore. The sun was shining when we started, with a few clouds - and 4 ft swells. Rob & Jesse both were at the Hull (Jim & I were, too), jumping, yelling and "Riding the Waves" The boat was really rocking! The whales would spout out the water, then a second later, you could see the huge ribbed back of the whale glide

SUBJECT & DATE   **NOTES**

through the waters surface.
We all saw a tail splash -
and we all saw the big
ribbed backs break the
waters surface.
The skipper knew where to
take the boat, and kept a
safe, respectful distance. He
would also get excited
about seeing the whales,
as we newcomers did.
Toward the end of the cruise,
it was getting cloudy,
to colder + windier. Jesse
and Rob went into the
cabin on the ride back to
the dock. Jesse fell asleep,
Rob dozed.

OBSERVATIONS

**SUBJECT
& DATE**

NOTES

ENTRIES

SUBJECT
& DATE

NOTES

OBSERVATIONS

**SUBJECT
& DATE**

NOTES

SUBJECT & DATE

N O T E S

OBSERVATIONS

**SUBJECT
& DATE**

NOTES

**SUBJECT
& DATE**

N O T E S

OBSERVATIONS

**SUBJECT
& DATE**

NOTES

**SUBJECT
& DATE**

N O T E S

OBSERVATIONS
NOTES

SUBJECT
& DATE

**SUBJECT
& DATE**

N O T E S

OBSERVATIONS

SUBJECT
& DATE

NOTES

SUBJECT & DATE	N O T E S
————	————————————————
————	————————————————
————	————————————————
————	————————————————
————	————————————————
————	————————————————
————	————————————————
————	————————————————
————	————————————————
————	————————————————
————	————————————————
————	————————————————
————	————————————————
————	————————————————
————	————————————————
————	————————————————
————	————————————————
————	————————————————
————	————————————————
————	————————————————
————	————————————————
————	————————————————
————	————————————————
————	————————————————
————	————————————————
————	————————————————

OBSERVATIONS
NOTES

**SUBJECT
& DATE**

**SUBJECT
& DATE**

N O T E S

OBSERVATIONS
N O T E S

**SUBJECT
& DATE**

**SUBJECT
& DATE**

N O T E S

OBSERVATIONS

NOTES

**SUBJECT
& DATE**

**SUBJECT
& DATE**

NOTES

OBSERVATIONS
N O T E S

**SUBJECT
& DATE**

**SUBJECT
& DATE**

N O T E S

OBSERVATIONS

**SUBJECT
& DATE**

NOTES

**SUBJECT
& DATE**

N O T E S

OBSERVATIONS

NOTES

**SUBJECT
& DATE**

SUBJECT & DATE **N O T E S**

OBSERVATIONS
NOTES

**SUBJECT
& DATE**

SUBJECT & DATE	NOTES

OBSERVATIONS

NOTES

**SUBJECT
& DATE**

**SUBJECT
& DATE**

N O T E S

OBSERVATIONS
NOTES

**SUBJECT
& DATE**

SUBJECT & DATE	NOTES

OBSERVATIONS
NOTES

**SUBJECT
& DATE**

SUBJECT & DATE	NOTES

OBSERVATIONS

**SUBJECT
& DATE**

NOTES

**SUBJECT
& DATE**

N O T E S

OBSERVATIONS

SUBJECT
& DATE

NOTES

ENTRIES

SUBJECT & DATE	NOTES

OBSERVATIONS

**SUBJECT
& DATE**

NOTES

SUBJECT & DATE **NOTES**

OBSERVATIONS
NOTES

SUBJECT
& DATE

**SUBJECT
& DATE**

N O T E S

OBSERVATIONS

**SUBJECT
& DATE**

NOTES

**SUBJECT
& DATE**

N O T E S

OBSERVATIONS

NOTES

**SUBJECT
& DATE**

ENTRIES

**SUBJECT
& DATE**

NOTES

OBSERVATIONS

NOTES

SUBJECT
& DATE

_____ _____
_____ _____
_____ _____
_____ _____
_____ _____
_____ _____
_____ _____
_____ _____
_____ _____
_____ _____
_____ _____
_____ _____
_____ _____
_____ _____
_____ _____
_____ _____
_____ _____
_____ _____
_____ _____
_____ _____
_____ _____
_____ _____
_____ _____
_____ _____
_____ _____
_____ _____
_____ _____

**SUBJECT
& DATE**

N O T E S

OBSERVATIONS
N O T E S

SUBJECT
& DATE

**SUBJECT
& DATE**

N O T E S

OBSERVATIONS

**SUBJECT
& DATE**

NOTES

**SUBJECT
& DATE**

N O T E S

OBSERVATIONS

NOTES

**SUBJECT
& DATE**

**SUBJECT
& DATE**

N O T E S

OBSERVATIONS

SUBJECT
& DATE

NOTES

SUBJECT & DATE   **N O T E S**

OBSERVATIONS

NOTES

**SUBJECT
& DATE**

**SUBJECT
& DATE**

N O T E S

OBSERVATIONS

SUBJECT
& DATE

NOTES

**SUBJECT
& DATE**

N O T E S

OBSERVATIONS
NOTES

**SUBJECT
& DATE**

**SUBJECT
& DATE**

N O T E S

OBSERVATIONS

**SUBJECT
& DATE**

NOTES

**SUBJECT
& DATE**

N O T E S

OBSERVATIONS

**SUBJECT
& DATE**

NOTES

_____ _____
_____ _____
_____ _____
_____ _____
_____ _____
_____ _____
_____ _____
_____ _____
_____ _____
_____ _____
_____ _____
_____ _____
_____ _____
_____ _____
_____ _____
_____ _____
_____ _____
_____ _____
_____ _____
_____ _____
_____ _____
_____ _____
_____ _____
_____ _____
_____ _____
_____ _____
_____ _____

**SUBJECT
& DATE**

N O T E S

OBSERVATIONS
NOTES

**SUBJECT
& DATE**

**SUBJECT
& DATE**

N O T E S

OBSERVATIONS
NOTES

**SUBJECT
& DATE**

SECTION 2

Birds
Wildlife
Plants   Trees
Seasonal Changes
Personal notes
Camera notes

B I R D S

DATE   NAME OF BIRD

NATURE LOVER'S LOG & JOURNAL

WILDLIFE

DATE   NAME OF ANIMAL

_____   _____

_____   _____

_____   _____

_____   _____

_____   _____

_____   _____

_____   _____

_____   _____

_____   _____

_____   _____

_____   _____

_____   _____

_____   _____

_____   _____

P L A N T S

DATE   NAME OF PLANT

_____   _____

_____   _____

_____   _____

_____   _____

_____   _____

_____   _____

_____   _____

_____   _____

_____   _____

_____   _____

_____   _____

_____   _____

TREES

DATE   NAME OF TREES

_____   _____

_____   _____

_____   _____

_____   _____

_____   _____

_____   _____

_____   _____

_____   _____

_____   _____

_____   _____

_____   _____

_____   _____

_____   _____

_____   _____

_____   _____

SEASONAL CHANGES

DATE   CHANGE NOTED

_____   _____

_____   _____

_____   _____

_____   _____

_____   _____

_____   _____

_____   _____

_____   _____

_____   _____

_____   _____

_____   _____

PERSONAL NOTES